FLOAT IN A WORDS

*Poems on Life,
Love and Loss*

By

Emma Walker

ISBN: 978-1-5272-5084-0
http://www.essexmeditation.co.uk/
http://www.essexcelebrantemma.co.uk/

DEDICATION

To my grandfather,
who instilled in me a deep and lasting love
for both words and the sea.

CONTENTS

Introduction

Funny things, poems.

Just words arranged in a few lines and yet somehow, so often more powerful, more evocative, more insightful than a couple of paragraphs might be. Less really is more.

I started writing poems in the course of my work as an Independent Funeral Celebrant. As part of this role, I interview bereaved families in preparation for writing and delivering a funeral script for the person they have lost. It's very important to me that funerals are personal, bespoke and according to the family's wishes, whatever they may be.

As part of this process I ask if they have a favourite poem or reading to be included in the funeral ceremony, and the bereaved family is often at a loss. Poetry is something to be venerated, only read at school under obligation and 'not for them'.

I understand what they mean. There are some overly sentimental, convoluted, rather wordy verses out there. So, I set out to write my own, inspired by individuals, by their lives, by their stories. For everyone has a story to tell. And these words were well received.

Once I began to build a collection of End of Life poems, Celebration of Life poems, other verses came swimming into view, for there is more to life than death.   Here presented for you is a collection of poetry, on love and loss and laughs, a sea of words, from my heart to yours.

Poems For The End Of Life

At that time which comes to us all, when our life on earth is over, what story will you leave behind? How will you be remembered, and who will tell your story? These first poems were written in exploration of the truth that life is more than just our last years. That we are all the result, the combination, of decades of experience: the good and the bad, light and shade, youth and maturity.

1. How To Remember

Remember me when I cannot
Remember how I was and what
I loved to do when I was young,
Vibrant, vivacious, full of fun

I danced all night, I swam in stars
I ran the race, I talked for hours
I never paused to think of what
Would happen, when my days grew short

I embraced my roles as wife and mother
On sunny days; through stormy weather
I was content with what life brought
I made it count, I gave it thought

I lived and laughed and loved and danced
I did it all, took up each chance
But then the clouds formed in my mind
A fog came down, no more sunshine

But through all this, you remembered me
Despite my changes, you still could see
The woman you had loved and known
Who gave you life, who made a home

Now that my life has drawn to a close
I hope that you will always know
I felt your love, throughout the years
So please, despite this time of tears

Remember me as once I was
Remember me, and then because,
your memory is strong and clear
It will be like I am still here.

2. Life In The Balance

It's easy to look back and judge
To see where you went wrong
But don't forget to count the times
That you were brave and strong

Mistakes are what we learn from
It's how we change and grow
But I regret, so many things
Much more than you could know

Our life on earth should be a time
Of love, of laughs and harmony
But human beings are sometimes prone
To anger or calamity

We want to spend our days in bliss
We try to be good friends
We work, we strive, we fall in love
Until one day, life ends

On that sad day our life is weighed
To see what tips the scales
Did our good and thoughtful deeds
Outweigh the times we failed?

It's easy to look back and judge
And say that I did wrong
But please recall the good times too
Now that I am gone

So take on board, learn, decide
Then when your own days cease
Those left behind will say of you
"He lived a life of peace".

3. My Hand In Yours

My hands once so tiny and soft
Held by your hands, so large and quite rough
I didn't know then, what had made them that way
Hard work, graft, labour, that kind of stuff

Your hardworking hands which brought in the cash
To ensure that our needs were well met
You did all you could, with all your might
To bring smiles and a roof overhead.

Now that those hands have ceased to work
You rest, but it feels wrong
How can my big, loving, crazy Dad
Be stopped? You were so strong

I cried when they told me
That you had passed away
And now it feels that I will cry
Each and every day

You may not have been the perfect Dad
You carried wounds and scars
You made mistakes, you made me cry
But I loved you Dad, I'm yours

Sometimes I needed you
You were not always there
And yet I think in your own way
In your own time, you cared

No more will I have the touch of
My soft hands in your rough fingers
And whatever we went through Dad
I want you to know that memory lingers

You loved me and I loved you
Proud to be my Daddy's girl
Rest those working hands Dad,
Find comfort, find peace, sleep well.

Like so many of her generation, the woman who inspired this poem had to stand up and face unexpected challenges. For young women like her, World War II often meant waving off their brothers, lovers and husbands to uncertainty overseas, and then getting on with their own lives on the Home Front. Coping with rationing, digging for victory, making do and mending, working in munitions factories and wondering if their children would grow up in a fatherless future. Truly remarkable for the so-called 'weaker sex' and I salute them.

4. A Remarkable Life

Your words, your deeds, your special way
The little things you used to say
Mother, grandmother and wife
All roles in your remarkable life

Not idly watching, but taking part
In life, in love, with all your heart.
Never one to quake in fear
You took a stand, and that we cheer

Nurturing each child in turn
Ensuring that good ways they'd learn
Guiding, caring, spending time
Always proud to say 'They're Mine'

In later years, though strength did wane
Your spirit held strong all the same
But one sad day you left us here
And we must tell you, Mother Dear

 "Remarkable" was the word for you
You influence each thing we do
Now that you've been called away
We miss you more than we can say.

My grandfather gave me many gifts. He took me out to sea, introducing me to the wind and waves, the joy of a billowing sail and salty lips. From the age of 5, each Saturday morning I would accompany him to the local library at the foot of the hill, there to carefully select my three books for the week. Ken the librarian would meticulously date stamp each volume and then off home we would trot, my grandfather and I, books tucked under our arms, each eagerly anticipating a long afternoon of losing ourselves in our newly discovered pages.

My grandfather died ten years ago, and I still miss him every day.

5. The Grandest Grandad

Parents are quite useful things
No life without Mum or Dad
But in my humble opinion
Better than parents, are those who are Grand

Grandparents are just more fun
And my Grandad's the best
You may think you have the winner
But my Grandad stands way above the rest

Right from the start he treasured me
I was his little star
He proudly told his listening chums
How I shone brightest by far

Sharing our own secret smile
We knew just what it meant
That we each adored the other
And together hours we'd spend.

My Grandad taught me games and rhymes
Showed me where treasure was found
My tiny, soft fingers were guided
By Grandad's weathered old hands

My Grandad told me I was able
To reach up to the sky
But now he's gone away from us
And I really want to cry

Instead I'll think of what he taught
And proudly here I stand
Saying thank you for being my Grandad
You were the best, such fun, just Grand.

6. A Gardener's Life

A green thumb and callused fingertips
An aching back and sun browned neck
This is what a garden brings

The hope of Spring with bud and blossom
Green shoots bringing life into one more year
This is the joy that a garden brings

A riot of colour, of scent, of delight
The high summer shouts of petals, purple and red
Cool, green grass carefully tended
Snatched shady naps under a tree
A gardener's life in full glory

Apples and blackberries, ripe for the picking
Falling leaves of amber and gold
Slower days as the sunlight dwindles
This too, a gardener's life

A robin perched on abandoned spade
Earth and leaf in deep hibernation
The gardener's life has seen its seasons
She now will rest, her task complete.

7. Rainbow Light

Somewhere over the rainbow
A place that's far away
Although we try to find it
Beyond our reach it stays

A land of dreams and bluebirds
That's how the old song goes
But what goes on in that far place
No-one really knows

We need to think that dreams come true
Else, what are dreams dreamt for?
The hopes and wishes that we send
Above the treetops soar

We'd rather you were home with us
For there's no place like home
But as that dream just can't come true
Over the rainbow you must go

We'll think of you as bathed in lights
Red, orange, yellow, green
Blue, indigo, and violet.
They'll soothe you as you dream

We never will forget you
Although we had to part.
Up in the sky, or rainbow's end
Yet deep within our hearts.

Not all babies are born. Some die before they reach the sun and air. But these babies are still their parents' children, still loved. Their futures have been imagined, their names have been chosen, their black and white images seen on that cherished ultrasound printout carried in a purse or wallet.
This poem honours these babies, and those who will always love them.

8. Small Blessing

One blessing of a life so short
Love is all that's found
No fear, no cold, no anger
Mum's heart the only sound
To be a tiny baby
Safe floating in its world
Knowing only warmth and care
Pure love around her swirls
We wish you had stayed longer
We wish you'd seen the sun
But we're so grateful, precious child
Your life was a peaceful one.

'Strictly Come Dancing' may have brought the magic of the ballroom into many young lives, but for previous generations, an evening of dancing at the Palais was an essential part of their weekend. Huddles of young men and women eyeing each other up from the edges of the dance floor, toes tapping to the sound of Victor Sylvester until a brave chap, doubtless egged on by his mates, approached one special young lady, and asked her to dance.

Sometimes that first dance led to a lifetime of love.

9. Ballad of the Ballroom

One enchanted evening
First glance across the floor
I took that step towards you
A quickstep, to be sure

To dance together was my dream
And sometimes dreams come true
You took my hand, I held you close
Wonderful waltzing with you

Side by side, cheek to cheek
Let's face the music and dance
Arm in arm, a partnership
Ours was a true romance

Now my earthly life is over
Those harps I can't ignore
I'll gladly rejoin my angel
Dance among the stars for evermore.

10. A Life of Laughs

It started with a smile across a crowded room
That twinkle in the eyes which was returned and soon
A dance of love was taken, each step around the
floor
A step towards a lifetime, of laughter, fun and more.

The first smile of your newborn, what joy that
moment brings
First step, first word, first haircut, pride in your child
begins
A little older, hide and seek and lots of other games
And when their small faces light up with mirth, yours
will do the same.

Jokes and teasing, puns and wit, always with a smile
Even though they're older now, at heart they're still a
child
As years go by, some tears will fall but there will be
more laughs
For this is a fine family that's strong and built to last.

And when the day you're dreading comes, when one
has passed away
When looking back across their life, you will be sure
to say

He was a man who loved us all, that memory is clear
He lived his life in happiness, indeed more laughs
than tears.

What is next, what do you think?

Do you have a vision of heaven, or are you convinced there is nothing more to life after death? Here are a few views for you to choose from.

11. What's Next?

When I am gone, I won't be here
My time will then be up
My smile will fade, some tears will fall
I'll bid goodbye to one and all
What's next we wonder, where do we go?
There's so much that we don't know

But does it matter? That's my thought

What's next for you who still remain?
Will you survive or feel the strain
I've no regrets, no wistful sighs
So there's no need to sob and cry
I've had my life, it was a blast
So there's no need to live in the past
Think of me then forward step
Your task?
To find out what is next.

12. My Kind Of Heaven

For me, I'd want to spend my days
Just strolling on the sands
Watch waves roll in and out again
Where ocean meets the land
Gazing at the far horizon
Clear sky and deep sea blend blues
Piercing cries of swooping gulls
Till sunset brings new hues
Soft pink and purple streak the clouds
Then velvet twilight falls
The stars shine soft above and yet
Toes in silver sand stay warm
The waves roll in and out again
The endless, ceaseless tides
But I'm at peace on this, my beach
To me, this is paradise.

13. Called Home

We never know when it will be,
That day when we're called home,
Our loves, our friends, may cling to us
But we must leave alone

We thank you for the time you spent
Brightening our lives
But time has come, you've been called home
And upwards you must rise

The clouds will part, the trumpets sound
Pure peace and rest you'll find
You've gone home, yet here on earth
You'll live on in our hearts and minds.

Poems For

Encouragement And Inspiration

14. Upwards

And we shall rise when we have fallen
No depth will be too far
We shall rise when we have almost
Lost our faith in who we are

We shall rise though some may falter
We believe in our own power
We shall rise although those worries on
Our shoulders weigh us down

Our confidence is built upon that inner strength we
found
Our belief has been hard won, tested, challenged,
been around
Only our own powers give us wings, upward thrust
and flight
Together we can rise up, we can soar to those new
heights

And we shall rise when we have fallen
No depth will be too far
We shall rise up, we will triumph,
That is who we are.

15. Just A Moment

It only takes a moment for everything to change
For life as once you knew it, to vanish in the haze
Just as life can start in a short moment of sheer bliss
Sometimes time is up before you realise what you'll
miss

It only takes a moment to tell others they are loved
To show your near and dearest the strong feelings
that you have
To talk about tomorrows, to reminisce about the past
To thank and praise, inspire or guide, say what's best
or worst

In just one single moment, dreams are lived or cruelly
crushed
The twist and turn of fate or chance, thus games are
lost and won
Some moments last a lifetime, while others fade at
once
Elastic time, recurrent thoughts, good deeds are left
undone

In this present moment, smile, breathe in and breathe
out
Note to self: Be Jolly and aim to make this moment
count
Peace be my companion in my last moment when it
comes
No regrets, no more to say, just gently journeying on.

16. Reflections

Wide expanse seeming without end
Blue, yet white, then blue again
Eyes wide open, wide open sky
Drifting, floating, the clouds and I

Swallows swoop and soar as one
They brush the earth, aim for the sun
Weightless, gravity defying, float
Immersed in blue above as below

Yet on my back, limbs spread wide
Gently carried by the tide
I feel as free as those swift birds
Floating in my sea of words.

17. Star Gazing

I am wishing on a star
That you will go far
I am wishing on a star
You'll be happy wherever you are

For you, my child, I wish big dreams,
For you, my child, I wish great things
Holding you in silver starlight,
I wish, I wish with all my might
That you, my child, will shine, will glow
That you, my child, real peace will know
That fear and hurt you will overcome
With confidence and inner wisdom
Wishing on a star for you
That my dreams and yours will all come true.

18. Life Is More Than A Journey

To each of us a life is given
To each a different path
To each of us our life is special
We know our own true worth

Inside our hearts, deep in our minds
We think, explore and play
Though life is more than a journey
We must learn along the way

Some of us stride far ahead
But some of us are shy
Some of us are slow to start
Who knows the reasons why

To each of us a life is given
But we don't live apart
We meet, we greet, we make a friend
We join hands, open our hearts

To each of us life is so special
A day, a week, a year
Who knows how long we have on earth
One day we won't be here

So let's embrace our differences
It's those that make us strong
Don't roll too fast along life's road
Make friends and bring them along.

19. Season's Greetings

May the sunlight which shines on you
Be a comfort to your bones
May the scent of grass and daisy chains
Be delightful to your nose
May longer days and shorter nights
Bring a lightness to your mind
May this summer be the season
When you leave your woes behind.

20. Three Wishes

When we wish upon a star, we hope our wish comes
true
But what we wish for most of all is that we still had
you
Your time has gone, you left our lives and now we all
gaze upwards
Watching for a bright, new star to take its place above
us

While with us, you lit up our world. Now soar up,
glow, shine, shimmer
A new star in the heavens, yet our loss will not grow
dimmer
We'll think of you each night at dusk as sunlight fades
away
A host of stars glow in the dark along the Milky Way

We wish upon your star, my dear, we wish and we
believe
In sweet dreams you will visit us but earth you had to
leave
So shine on, send your starlight, many hope and have
faith too
That when they wish upon your star, their dreams will
all come true.

Love

So mysterious, so infuriating, so addictive, so all-consuming, so wonderful.

I wrote this poem on the back of an envelope one rainy afternoon whilst sitting in my car waiting for 3 o'clock to strike. Just like true love, poetry can pop up at the most unexpected times and places.

21. United

I loved you in the morning
When you strolled into my life
I loved you in the evening
When I pledged to be your wife

The magic which I felt that day
That spell has never broken
We stopped, we stared, you smiled
No words needed to be spoken

For us the circle was complete
We asked for nothing more
Within our joint embrace, my love
Peace, passion, strength: mine and yours

You filled my heart with summertime
Shared soft kisses every day
Even in those darker hours
You knew just what to say

I love you and I always will
I know that you love me
Soulmates, lovers, entwined for life
United we'll always be.

22. Yours Sincerely

I like the neatness of a letter
You know exactly where you are
Beginning, middle, ending
Then sent to near or far

You start with Dear, and end with Love
Each sentence carefully planned
There's time to think, and write again
I like the post, it's real life I can't stand.

When someone is your penpal
You send them all your best,
Best words, best side, best wishes
You can hide away the rest

You can hide your messy thoughts and deeds
The stuff you'd rather ignore
Feelings, worry, loneliness
Anger, pain, hope and more

By post, or these days all online,
Friends, suitors - they're not that close
And so I can take my own sweet time
Then flirt with those I like the most

I want to say I love you
To my daughters and my sons
But to these truly loved ones
That phrase rarely comes

It's not that I don't feel or care
I just prefer to type or write
Face to face, confusion reigns
Although I try with all my might

At last, I'll write a letter
To read when I've gone above
'Darling' it starts, 'Forever Yours' it ends
My secret, deepest love.

This big blue and green planet we are all hitching a ride upon has much to delight and sustain us. If we are lucky enough to be surrounded by mountains, forest or field then fresh air and fortitude are ours for the taking. But for more urban dwellers, a moment in our garden, or lunch break on a park bench can do wonders to re-green our minds, to invigorate our senses, to bring us back to earth.

23. I Love To Tend My Garden

I love to tend my garden
To watch it bloom and grow
From bulbs or seeds or cuttings
Each little plant I know

Pretty petals, lush green grass
Apples, plums and pears
Fragrant lilies; red, red rose
Beauty everywhere

My garden is a joy to me
I spend there happy hours
But this green space not just for me
I think of it as ours

My family, both young and old
Can play and dance and run
Upon the lawn, beneath the trees
Fresh air and full of fun

On quieter days I sit and watch
As raindrops gently fall
And think how much my garden
Brings joy to one and all

I love to tend my garden
Flowers - pink and blue
Butterflies and honey bees
A most delightful view.

24. My Beautiful Butterfly

The beauty of the butterfly is in its pair of wings
So delicate, so fragile, such a lovely thing.
Emerging from a drab cocoon, into the morning sun
First spreads its wings, and then takes flight, journey
just begun.

The butterfly will spend its days visiting the flowers
Sipping nectar, gentle dance, is how it fills the hours
Swallowtail, Chalk Hill Blue, Red Admiral, Small
White
Peacock, Monarch, Small Tortoiseshell, each name is
a delight.

Marigold and lavender, hollyhocks and daisies
Orange, purple, pink and white; the colours are
amazing
How charmed a life for butterfly, to flit from flower
to flower
Without a care, with all the grace that nature will
allow her.

Through Spring and Summer butterfly is nature's
beauty queen
Entrancing colours, enchanting flight, a sight that
must be seen.

And if one friendly butterfly should rest upon your knee
Your face lights up, your spirits soar, your heart has been set free.

25. The River

Always there, yet ever changing
My river flows on by
The sparkling, rippling, green, brown ribbon
Beneath the clear blue sky

A rustle in far bulrushes
Small troop of coots appears
The soft wind plays in the willows
Long weeping branches sway beside the weir

Water gloops as brown trout leaps
To capture daily mayfly
Quiet on the bank, an angler poised
To reel in or recast with small sigh

This river always changing
Endless flow from source to sea
Observing from my riverbank
Where I'm content to be.

26. Family Tree

This tree has seen many winters, weathered many storms
Cracked bark has felt weak sun upon those frosty dawns
Ancient roots held firm, their place in earth steadfast
Drawing moisture from the soil, and nutrients for life

Those roots run deep, reaching far underground
Supporting gnarled, tall trunk: twelve feet around
A ring for each year, strength builds within
Of all the trees in the wood, this mighty oak is King

Ever upwards, reaching skyward, each Spring growth anew
Each bud, each leaf, each acorn, a sign for me and you
For this tree is our family; established, grounded, loved
Cherished, respected, valued. A tree that should be hugged.

27. A Woman's Best Friend

My favourite friends have kindly eyes
That shine when we are meeting
The kind of friend who's glad to hear
'Good Boy!' as a fond greeting.

When out about, I meet new friends
Town or country, both the same
I stop and stoop and pat their head
Asking them 'and what's your name?'

Pug, Jack Russell, Labrador
Yorkie, poodle, Pekingese
Mongrel, stray or pedigree
My heart is lost to all the breeds

People can be a funny lot
Not always playing fair
But with a favourite canine friend
I know what's what. They care

I know that funny, furry face
Will light up when I'm home
A hairy head upon my knee
With my mutt, I'm never alone.

Some say that it's a dog's life
That seems ok to me
But life without a shaggy dog
How boring that would be

My favourite friends are furry
And sometimes muddy too
Side by side, for miles and miles
Loyal, trusting and true

To me the lighter side of life means cake, biscuits, sports, perhaps a trip to the pub and always having an eye out for a bargain.

28. A Sweet Life

It started with a biscuit
And then a Crunchie bar
Delicious Cherry Bakewell
Mr Kipling, you're a star!

Custard creams, almond slice
Rose pink Turkish Delight
Perhaps you could manage another?
Oh, I think I might.

But for a truly sweet, sweet life
It takes more than cherry tart
For sweetness is a part of some
Deep down within their heart

Kind words, a smile, thoughtfulness
These are the things that you possess
For you showed us, right from the start
Much better than cake, is your sweet heart.

29. Public House And Second Home

A swift half at the Rose and Crown
My usual at the Bell
Sink a few at the Dog and Duck?
Cheers! I might as well

First left at the Eagle, then
Turn right by the Woodman's Arms
Both hostelry and landmark,
These pubs have double charms

The regulars prop up the bar
That's where they're always found
Drink till they no longer know
Just whose *is* that next round

Red Lion, Swan or Royal Oak
White Hart or other name
From Rising Sun to Traveller's Rest
You're welcome all the same.

30. Playing A Round

Now sitting in this clubhouse
I have some time on hand
To think about my life in golf
I really am a fan

'A good walk spoiled' is what some say
'What rubbish!' I respond
What else could fill your heart with joy
Than greens to putt upon

It's true that golf can sometimes be
Confusing, cold or wet.
It's Birdie, Eagle, Albatross
How strange can jargon get?

A double bogey, slice, the yips
Wedge, bunker, iron and swing
And here's a time where "under par"
Is seen as a good thing.

But standing on the 18th tee
Where games are lost and won
I look along the fine fairway
And worries have I none

Fresh air, good friends, a well-kept green
And nature all around
A better game than golf, it seems
For me just can't be found

And when we reach the 19th hole
And tot up all the scores
Win or lose, the cry goes up
'It's not my round, it's yours'.

31. Yellow Sticker

Yellow Sticker hour is looming
Seems my best has all gone before
Clock is ticking and time's running out
I'm due to be shown the door
My place is now next to bagged salad
With wilting, slimy pea shoots and leaves
Just who is it buys that revolting rotting mess
Even if reduced to 50p?

Once I was fresh, hot from the oven
And special, with cranberries and seeds
But I loafed about, now I'm drying out
Save me! This is my plea
Behold, my bright yellow sticker
Take me home, holding me tight
Then you know the drill, put me under the grill
Hot buttered toast, what a delight.

Loss comes in many forms. Perhaps we are grieving for one who has died. Maybe our heart is broken, for our true love has turned out to be a traitor. Regardless of the cause, loss hurts, and continues to hurt long after the headlines have faded, long after the sympathy of our friends has dried up.
Time is a healer they say, I'm not really convinced of that. I think we just get better at dealing with the gaping hole in our lives as each day passes.

32. Every Cloud Has A Silver Lining

When the raindrops start to splash and fall
I stop what I'm doing, and head for the hall
Pull on that coat which hangs on the hook
Stride out the front door, without a backwards look

Left at the end of the garden path
Now almost running, I'm walking so fast
All that I need is the blessing of rain
It covers, it hides, my outpouring of pain

For I need to cry, I want to wail
Tears build up inside me on gargantuan scale
Time hasn't healed, nor dulled my grief
I feel no longed for comfort, nor sense of relief.

Under my own roof, I must smile and pretend
For the people I live with, I don't wish to offend
But, oh, for the freedom to face the pouring rain
And pretend they are raindrops, these searing tears of
pain.

33.   247365

It's twenty four seven
Day after endless day
There isn't a minute
When pain goes away

How can I go forward?
My heart is torn in two
The only thought in my head
Is You,
You,
You

We shared deepest secrets
We were always in step
But now I am stumbling
I feel like a wreck

24/7 x 52
Each and every moment
I'll be missing you.

34. Missing

It's the lack
The space
The absence
The 'to do' list that's all done
The quiet of an evening
It's the phone that hasn't rung
The junk mail keeps arriving
They don't know you've gone
That hollow in the cushion
Glasses perched next to your chair
Jar of green olives in the fridge
Red coat left hanging on the stairs
Single mug of strong black coffee
No more weak Earl Grey tea
This peaceful home
Once me and you
Too quiet for me
Just me.

35. Your Loss, My Pain

Moment by moment, breathing in and out
Minute by minute, watch that clock ticking round
Left foot then right foot, one step at a time
When loss comes a calling, light is hard to find

Moment by moment, dull pain weighs you down
Minute by minute, relentless aching heart
Left foot then right foot, you drag yourself around
Loss leaves you listless, if you're the one who's left
behind.

Downturned page in the paperback, now no longer
read
Dent left in the pillow, empty space in bed
Weathered waxed jacket left hanging in the hall
Familiar, tender outline impressed in them all

The heartache of absence, the loneliness of loss
Confusion, depression, my grief for what once was,
Moment by moment, must breathe in and breathe out
Where love once lived, now loss squats, breaking my
aching heart.

36. What If?

Do you ever pause to wonder what would happen
If you stepped off from the edge?
If all would cease, bleak darkness fall, who would
notice at all
Your descent from that high ledge.
Do you ever ponder why your life is such a mess
Why past years lay discarded, tossed aside, toxic with
regret?
Do you ever contemplate which path you'll end up
taking?
And will that route meander, bypass, muddle or
deceive
Destination still unknown, till misadventure breaks
you
Reeling, battered, bruised and struggling to breathe

Me?
I cogitate, consider, mull it over all the time
Deciphering the ceaseless, muddied churnings of my
mind
So what do I discover, do enlightenment I find?
That seed of doubt, brief glimpse of joy, a spark of
light within
Which causes me to pause, to hope, to not bloody give in

To all the darkness round about, the slime, the sludge,
the dregs
Though life sometimes feels too much, we're all a
long time dead.
Choose life.

37. Choptank

We hold our breath, just hoping
That things will be OK
Fingers crossed, invoking gods
That all will go our way
In trepidation, with trembling limbs
We inch out on the stage
For we are merely players
Who try to act our age

Countless opportunities
To rise, to fall, to lie
Somehow mostly muddling through
Not winning, just getting by
We had great expectations
But that was long ago
When we were sure of who we were
knew all there was to know
But now that great revelation comes
The sharpest truth of all
The more we learn, the less we know
As our world grows, we feel small

Perhaps it's better to be stuck
In cosy, snug delusion
Than break out into the wide new world
Unknown, uncertainty, full of confusion
For me I'd rather be unsure
And brave that road not travelled
With high hopes, chance, an open mind
Some stumbles, yet destined to dazzle.

And finally …

Just as there is so often an unsung hero or heroine who is the power behind the throne, alongside most authors and poets is a person who has ears. Each line of verse in this collection has been heard first by my husband, Mr Walker. He has never failed to listen, respond and react; for better or worse, in sickness and in health.

All he asked for in return was a poem of his own.

38. For Mr Walker, Who Wanted
A Poem Of His Own

You never know what you will find
Deep within a person's mind
The outer shell is there to hide
All wonders that may dance inside

That bloke who's driving his white van
Is thoughtful and insightful
His head's full of philosophy
His garden is delightful.

Just as a three piece suit may clothe
Full body tatts and piercings,
'Neath shaven head and workman's hands
There beats good heart unceasing

When next you wonder, 'Why her and him?'
Perhaps you'll pause to ponder
What treasure is contained within
With what fine mind he won her.

ABOUT THE AUTHOR

Emma Walker grew up on the mudflats of Essex then took flight once she was old enough, spending the next twenty years travelling the world. She made a life for herself in the Rocky Mountains of Colorado, the bustling city of Washington DC, the depths of the French forest, in the shadow of the Himalayas in Nepal and the confusion of Taipei before returning to settle in Essex.

When she is not writing poems on the back of envelopes, Emma works as an Independent Funeral Celebrant, leading funeral services which reflect the life of the deceased, allowing them to leave the world in the way they lived.

During her travels around the world, Emma was fortunate enough to study with many Buddhist masters, and spent years in meditative retreat. She now shares her meditation experiences in local classes, her style is practical, down to earth and friendly.

Happily married to Mr Walker, Emma also shares her home with two stepchildren, two step-dogs and an ever multiplying tribe of fish in the garden pond.

http://www.essexmeditation.co.uk/
http://www.essexcelebrantemma.co.uk/